T0351954

THE  BRAZILLER  SERIES  OF  AUSTRALIAN  POETS

# The Deep North

*a selection of poems by*

# B R O N W Y N   L E A

WITH A NOTE BY PAUL KANE

GEORGE BRAZILLER / NEW YORK

This Project has been assisted by the Australian Government through the Australia
Council for the Arts, its arts funding and advisory body.

George Braziller, Inc.
277 Broadway, Suite 708
New York, NY 10007

Library of Congress Cataloging-in-Publication Data
Lea, Bronwyn, 1969–
[Poems. Selections]
The deep north : a selection of poems / by Bronwyn Lea ; with a note by Paul Kane.
—First edition.
        104 pages cm.— (The Braziller Series of Australian Poets)
ISBN 978-0-8076-1626-0
I. Title.
PR9619.4.L43A6 2013
821'.92—dc23
2013024113

First edition
Designed by Rita Lascaro
Printed in the United States of America

# TABLE OF CONTENTS

*"I promise you I solve nothing."*

Toward the end of *The Deep North*, Bronwyn Lea writes of her childhood in Papua New Guinea, "I will survive // but not fully recover" ("Port Moresby"). That gap between survival and recovery opens up the possibility—and for her, the necessity—of poetry, for poems are themselves modes of recovery, attempts at the recuperation (the "getting again") of experience. "It will all happen here," she goes on to say, in the words on the page and in the blank spaces between them. These persistent gaps are not static but generative and dynamic because they resist closure and respond to the constantly changing circumstances of life—a life, in her case, of movement, of covering distances. Lea's journeys take us to Queensland, California, Colorado, Peru, India, Sri Lanka, Papua and Paris. Travel, of course, is always displacement and it functions here as an image of inward dislocation as well; in "Driving into Distance" Lea recounts a failure of intimacy, of the fear undermining an *I-Thou* relation:

> Language,
> it seems, misrepresents me: the *I* bending
> its tyranny into an argillaceous loop, running
> circles around desire, until the self is a Mobius
> strip and *I love you* a cruel equation equaling
> a snowdrift between us.

So many of Lea's poems detail failures of this sort that one expects a poetry of despair or bitterness, of a wounded and wounding irony that defends the self against an impinging world. What we get, instead, is something closer to celebration, an embracing of desire, where passion, sensuality and eroticism are fully present:

> what can she do, she has opened
> her eyes as he balanced above her
>
> bent down to kiss her mouth
>
> what can she do, she has opened
> she has opened.
>     ("Routine Love Poem")

Even the natural world is complicit in this, as we see in "Love Begins with a Vision":

> think of a swallow's wheeling
>     flight flaring out
> like a flamenco dancer's skirt.

The strength of Lea's vision is precisely this capacity not to transcend suffering ("there is no language // of the holy") but rather to work through it in the "vernacular of the natural world" ("Ordinary Grace"). It is in her determined attendance upon the world that Lea discloses herself as a phenomenologist of the heart. There is first the heart's knowledge:

> There is a man I know with eyes heavy
> with sand and sometimes sullen blue like
> the haze of the eucalypt grove that makes
> you remember all the f-words you never use
> like *forgiven* and *forever*.

which is then elaborated through tropes:

> He has grown on me
> like an embryo until without him I feel thrown
> into being incomplete like the wintering
> rose bush de-leafed and out of bloom;

and fused in an image both external and inner, "like this falling apart mountain, a mountain / that all my tying together won't mend" ("Antipodes"). Lea stays close to the contours of experience because that is the ground of her understanding, the means whereby she moves and is moved. In a poem that picks up (and takes apart) Thomas Parnell's eighteenth-century bromide, "The Hermit," where an angel rises to "strangle his host's infant son" because, as Parnell puts it, "God, to save the Father, took the Son," Lea reimagines a similar scene where a husband is bereft:

> What if the man, looking up
> from his pain, saw tears in the eyes of an angel
> and, unflinching, reached out,
> as nightly he reached out to his children,
> filled not with forgetting but deep remembering,
> his body flowing with a tenderness not to be found
> in books or false sermons, but the fierce
> tenderness of one who will give everything to survive.
>     ("The Angel and the Hermit")

As Shelley says in "A Defence of Poetry," "The great secret of morals is love; or a going out of our nature." Lea has that poetic capacity to imagine and identify with the other, even (with "fierce tenderness") those who have caused her pain, as in "Born Again," when an ex-husband returns—having found religion—and is discovered praying on his knees under a ponderosa pine "weighted with snow":

> Snow drifts
> on his shoulder and backs of his shoes.
> Snow collected on his upturned palms.
> I felt its coldness. Such intimacy

we had never shared. Sometimes grace
comes like that, it falls like snow.

That Lea recognizes this as a moment of grace for them both attests
to a facility for radically altering her perspective, which, in turn,
gives her access to both ecstasy (literally, "standing outside oneself")
and humor. In leading us through a "way out of the insufferable /
medium of a par-boiled heart," she tells us she will be waiting out
back of the theater of the self: "I'll be the one who is smiling" ("The
Other Way Out"). There is something amiable about this poetry
that belies the harsh knowing Lea has endured, but such geniality is
as much a result of suffering as it is its inversion, for it stems from
a deep acceptance of what her life has been and is. This, as much as
anything, accounts for the honed diction and the plain speaking of
the verse. Robert Frost, in "Education by Poetry," holds that "Poetry
provides the one permissible way of saying one thing and meaning
another." That duplicity (as it so often is with Frost) is something
Lea eschews in her "Ars Poetica":

> I used to want
> to say one thing
>
> & have it turn
>
> out to be another.
> Now I only want
>
> to say one thing.
> As if the pleasure
>
> now is in the voicing
> not the trickery
>
> but the soul making
> itself heard
>
> above the traffic.

That "voicing," that wish to be heard despite the cacophony of our contemporary signal-to-noise ratio, is the true accomplishment of *The Deep North*, for the poems get lodged in our ear and under our skin. We are surprised—which is to say "seized"—by this voice, this poetry, as it makes its way out of the deep north, that antipodean transposition (for us), whereby dislocation and difference—like the tropical heat of Queensland—peel away the orthodox formalities and formidable distances that might otherwise hold us back from returning the warm embrace proffered here.

—Paul Kane

THE DEEP NORTH

# Born Again

After the divorce he sold his house
by the beach and drove his Volkswagen
into the desert to die. He was gone
a year. I was living one vertical mile
above the desert floor—where he slept
in his car—in a house that overlooked
a great sweep of rocks and woodlands.
Instead of dying, god spoke to him.
God forgave all of his trespasses. But I
didn't forgive his trespasses against me.
My heart was a long ledger. One day
he returned to collect our daughter.
My house was snowbound. I left him
to stand in the weather while I gathered
her things. It took a little while. When
I returned he was gone. Typical.
I looked around. Sparrows scratched
at the snow looking for seeds. I saw
a figure kneeling by a large granite
boulder. The ponderosa above him
was weighted with snow. The knees
of his jeans were wet. Snow drifts
on his shoulders and backs of his shoes.
Snow collected on his upturned palms.
I felt its coldness. Such intimacy
we had never shared. Sometimes grace
comes like that, it falls like snow.

# The Other Way Out

One way out of the insufferable
medium of a par-boiled heart

is to desire desire until your lungs
expand like a universe

light years away from implosion.
Forget this wanting a little a lot

of things (or its converse), aim
to want it all—the red dress, red shoes

the body with its yellow fat and red
muscle shifting your mysterious bones.

Another way out is to exhale,
to toss everything until you are left

with only a desire to toss things out—
get rid of that, too. Tell the world

it can't fire you because you've quit,
say *Self, sit till you no longer want*

*to blaze in paradise.* Stand in
the corner until each thought is

a fly crawling across the white wall
of your flesh. Whether

you walk the ascetic alley—
barefoot on the dead tufted earth

or gape inside the rococo theater—
your hands parting the velvet curtain

step out, step through, meet me
out back. I'll be the one who is smiling.

## Antipodes

In this lifetime *antipodes* must be my word,
my home or anyone else's. Anyone who lives
at opposites or knows what it is to be contrary,
to deviate. Like disparate continents.
Like the holding of Europe and Australia
in your blood. This, I find, is a feat.
And I recognize as I age that my apogees
are elongating, my reversals are rising
like the swollen belly of a frog storing water
in its sleep. My friend feels it too and wonders
if she can ever love down to the lonely and beyond;
beyond that rocky, existential space that women
like us, so schooled in ricochet, retreat from
with the swiftness of a silver-capped bullet.
There is a man I know with eyes heavy
with sand and sometimes sullen blue like
the haze of the eucalypt grove that makes
you remember all the f-words you never use
like *forgiven* and *forever*. He has grown on me
like an embryo until without him I feel thrown
into being incomplete like the wintering
rose bush de-leafed and out of bloom;
like the falling apart mountain, a mountain
that all my tying together won't mend.
Then just now, lying in the low light
of afternoon, I saw it is the movement
more than the man that I love; the movement
in and out of me, framing the sweet falling
of lilac pollen, falling soft upon his back,
my tongue.

# A Place

There is a place I like to go
that is behind language

I like to go there and wobble
like a melon on a table

or a spoon that doesn't care
if it is chosen or not

I also like to come back
and slip into "myself"

like a pair of silk pajamas
ornamental and cool to touch.

## Bronwyn Lea

As Maureen O'Hara did, my mother named
her daughter after Anna Lee's Bronwyn Morgan
from *How Green Was My Valley*. I like to think

she did not know the burden she was inflicting
with a name meaning *white breast*—from the Welsh
*braun* meaning *fleshy* and *gwen* meaning *blessed*—

the metaphor was lost on schoolboys who came
up with more vulgar translations. Australian boys
hadn't heard of Branwen, daughter of King Llyr,

sent to Ireland to marry Matholwch, then banished
to the kitchen as a slave, her ears boxed daily
by the butcher—though if they had, I like to think

the boys might have been more gallant. Branwen
taught a starling to speak and sent it to Wales
to tell her brother Bran of her plight. His army

sailed to Ireland to rescue her, where a bloody battle
broke out: two kingdoms destroyed on her account,
Branwen fled to Aber Alaw and died of grief. Lea

means *meadow*—perhaps the one where Branwen was
buried—else a set of warp threads carried by a loop
of the heddle. Swopping vowels, *lee* is a place

sheltered from the wind, and back in Wales *lli*
becomes a stream. Always in the plural, *lees* is dregs—
as employed by Macbeth to himself on the state

of his soul: *Renown and grace is dead,*
*The wine of life is drawn, and the mere lees*
*Is left this vault to brag of.*

Said quickly, my name is an adverb: attached
to action so as to qualify it—as in, to travel *bronwynly*
which might be to travel within an ace of salvation

or to survive exile and die the first night home.
But it is my first not last name that leaps from the page—
I like to think it is my true family's name: Branwen

my foremother—ears bruised, pale breast exposed
to the pale Welsh sun—she walks upstream, leaving
no footprints, her vowels mutating through the years

her consonants and grief her only constants. She stares
at me—as a hunter stares down a deer—and smiles.
My name fits me perfectly as the arrow fits its wound.

# How to Become a Fossil

Best to live and die on a flood plain
close to a meandering river.

Best to die in a place you'll be buried
by silt, mud or windblown sand.

A lakeshore or a migrating sand dune.
Best to sink in quicksand

or be trapped in tar. Best to be buried
before the sun can dissolve

your bones. Best to die in a burrow,
hidden from scavengers,

best to be colonized by maggots,
ants, beetles, wasps, best to bloom

with fungi, a swamp of bacteria
to polish your bones. Best to die alone

without burial rites or soul-transporting
ceremonies. Best to inter in a layer

of limestone, your bones
encased as you descend deeper

and deeper into history. Best to mineralize
quickly, within fifty millennia,

ground water creeping into your pores
to hang crystals on the walls

of your cells. Best to erode
in the heart of an arid land bereft

of topsoil or vast vegetation,
far from earthquakes that might twist

and fracture, or turn your stone
bones to ash. Best to be seen

by eyes eager to see what you meant
to keep hidden, to be held

by hands that will tend you,
as in life you had hoped to be tended—

with patience, wonder, an exactitude
approaching love—all that is you

but not you under downlights:
your inner self on permanent display.

# Women of a Certain Age

Women of a certain age are waking up
in the middle of things—birth and death feel
blessedly far away—the raw edge of real
departure and arrival a distant memory,
days fleeting in restful harmony like leaves
seen through a window—drifting
with all the others until they are reimagined
again by light, time and rain. Women
of a certain age are waking to the sound
of their breathing which through the long dark
hours has frightened them. In their worry
to light up a few inches of the universe,
a fraction of the infinite, however minute,
they are waking before dawn to witness
a victory of light, the capture of every trench
of shadow. The dawn will be theirs to hold
a little while—its lightness—they will forget
some of what they have experienced
and remember what they were born with,
including that which is too early to remember.
Women of a certain age—loving this
lightness—are rolling onto their sides,
rising out of their beds and out of their bodies,
imagining themselves free of the earth
and its drive to replace them, they are speeding
like comets over the edge of the universe,
falling and flying out of the familiar,
plummeting into the unknown to arrive
at a new hospitable household, having slipped
away without goodbyes, only smoke
as they burn—bluer and bluer—on the last
drop of fuel to be found only in the bodies
of women of a certain age.

# The Dream

You enter through a wedge of black
pushing slowly along the bottom of the canvas—
anchor, skirt, pedestal: the black
is solid yet lets all forms remain open.
From the black you are deposited into the flux
of the woman's body. Her left arm,
like the wing of a hatchling, is awkward
as in sleep. The woman changes
into an egg, apparition & seashell—
her body into sea & sky, her eye
into a bird. Yellow spills
from the cracked shell of her torso as if
breath or pillow or flame
that keeps the dream burning. The woman's right
arm, like an archway, opens into the distance
as if she is swimming or flying or falling,
afloat on a dream drawing toward the horizon—
translucent, billowing like a sail,
she swells & snaps & rolls
from flat plane to volume. She pushes
against the frame, shedding the lines
that define her & rises like a hot air balloon,
pulling you along with her.

# Orthograde

I have pictured her from the back,
a curving coming down the spine,
through the hip and then reversing
to a graceful S-bend
as it travels down the weight-bearing foot.
A figure standing contrapposto,
a plumb line dropped from the base of the neck,
the upward hip-swing exaggerated,
the matching shoulder slightly dropped.

A life contoured with a fine stick
of willow charcoal,
an Ingres envelope of living,
a nude with all its lines and glances
adding up to a faint facsimile of god.
I say, "your eye sockets
are midpoint on your face, your beauty
pronounced in the curvature
of your mouth, your head surprisingly deep,"
as if by recounting the lines
I might be excluded from their mystery.
And though what my eye follows is the form,
the pubis reproduced with its soft assertion,
I cannot see the pelvic bone,
stacked like a high-backed saddle,
a scaffolding for some ancient plan.
Yet I know it is the unseen
that is the principle thing.

I'm most unstable when upright,
dizzy with each unfolding complication
of walking—the deliberate displacement
of balance—the continual loss
and recapture. But in running
I've known the moment
when both feet are off the ground,
momentum thrusting even further forward,
balance point always leading,
heedless of the requisite fall.

# Seven Feet & Where They're From

*1   The Greek Foot*

Nature in her wisdom has formed the human feet
so they stand at the very bottom of the body.

The feet—or let us say foot—divides into three:
the seats of fortune, refinement and fate respectively.

The profile of the foot is wedge-shaped, with the crest
running in line with the big toe, and the plane of

the foot slopes down to the flat at the outer edge.
The weight-bearing arch disperses the body's weight

through the big toe, and the other toes fan out to
stabilize the balance. At the opposite end,

the heel is not directly under the ankle, but
projects backward so that the line running down

the calf through the Achilles tendon bulges slightly.
Socrates said when our feet hurt we hurt all over.

## 2  *The Chinese Foot*

The bandage wraps figure eights
around her heel, across the crest
of her foot and tightly over her toes
(which are black and pressed
to her sole) so that her arch breaks
magnificently with the steep pitch
of a temple. She lets her husband
touch it. He uses the measure
of his thumbtip-to-first-knuckle
along her lily foot and counts one,
two, three, and smiles. He brings it
to his lips, inhales, and thanks
the ancestors, who also smile
and wish him many sons. He has
loved her since first he saw her,
swaying in the courtyard like
a little tree, her long braid blue
under the moon, her lily feet
dressed in green apple silk shoes.
His mouth fell open at the sight,
but he was careful when he
exhaled not to blow her over
with the white cloud of his breath.

### 3  The Portuguese Foot

Her feet are the same ivory
color as the lit candle balanced
on her head.

She leans against the lagar
looking reluctant
but this, you learn, is only shyness

and this she forgets
when she begins to sing. She sings
in that plaintive,

strident voice that is the singing
voice of all Portuguese women, the bare
backs of her knees

pressing against the cold
granite wall, cold grapes rolling
under her feet. You expect

the grapes to crush
easily but they are resistant.
Only gradually does the juice spurt

between her toes and stain
her ivory feet. And when you look
at the tumbled sea

of fruit that she must tread
the labor seems Herculean and the human
foot too frail.

## 4  *The Indian Foot*

The *mehendiwalli* sifts the twigs and stems
from the ground henna leaves

and soaks it in a decoction of nilgiri oil,
tea, lemon juice and sugar

to make a thick paste. She rolls plastic
sheets into cones and fills them

with spoonfuls of henna paste. She paints
floral vines, paisleys and lace-like

lines onto the bride's soles. Letters
of the groom's name are hidden

in the flowers. On their wedding night
the bride will ask the groom to search

for the letters of his name. If he finds
them he will dominate his bride. If

he cannot the bride will dominate
her groom. As she waits for her feet to dry

what keeps the bride from cheating? From
accidentally smearing a letter or two?

## 5  The Aboriginal Foot

One day a Kuniya rock python
woman walked one thousand years
to the great shade of Uluru. She
travelled with her eggs nested
on her head in a grass *manguri*,

and when she arrived at the eastern
end of the rock, she buried her
eggs in the red sand. Later, she was
attacked by a Liru poisonous snake
warrior. She killed the warrior

with her digging stick, and his eyes,
head wounds and severed nose
can be seen on the western face of
the cliff. The woman's features
are preserved on the eastern face

of the gorge, and her story is
preserved in a dance at the base
of the red rock, her daughter's feet
dragging through the sand to leave
the meandering tracks of a snake.

6   *The American Foot*

The anatomical narrative takes
the hand of the physician and
guides it through a dissection

of the cadaver's sole: the narrative
opens with the foot placed on a
high block, the sole uppermost

and firmly secured, and proceeds
with an incision carried round
the heel and along the inner and

outer borders of the foot to the
great and little toes. The incision
should divide the integument

and the thick layer of granular
fat so that the fascia is visible.
The narrative concludes with

the sole peeled in a direction
from the heel forward to expose
the foot's inner workings. The

sole thus detached, the narrative
is hailed "a masterpiece, a best
seller, the *Summa* in its field."

7   *The Etymological Foot*

1)  Between the varied current
        senses of a word like *foot*
    there is often a family

                resemblance to
            suggest a common origin.

2)  The Latin *pes*, a foot,
    akin to the Greek *pous*,

            has an adjective *pedalis*,
        whence the English *pedal*,

            of the foot (or feet).

3)  *Repudium*, a back-footing,
    a rejection indicated by pushing

            back with the foot,

    especially a rejection of a wife
    by her husband.

4)  *Impedire*, to put someone's feet
    in shackles, hence to prevent

    from walking
                or to *impede*.

5)  *Impedicare*, to tangle someone's feet
    in a trap, hence fetter,

which yields to *impeach,*
     to charge with an official crime
or misdemeanor.

6) In folk etymology,
   *repudium* is related to

     *me pudet,*
     I am ashamed.

7) *Expedire,* to free one's feet
   from shackles,

     from which we get
     *expedentia,* an advantage,
     an opportunity,

   and *expedition,*
   originally a freeing
     which yields to *expeditious,*
     prompt.

8) One day I walked
   a long time alone.
   I abandoned the search for ultimate truth
   and took
   tutelage in putting one foot
   before another.

## These Gifts

Days like these—cool afternoons
in late summer, a rain so delicate
you can sit in the backyard and let the mist
drizzle your face. There's no grass
of course. A late heat wave has bleached
the lawn, burnt off the last of the tree ferns.
Just last week children and the elderly
were suffering from heatstroke. Yet
these gifts that arrive late season—
an apology you hadn't dared hope for,
a rush of poems, an impromptu patience
with the world. You rest your head
against a silky oak, and by your cheek
two butterflies coupled in flight
sex it up. And the day has charmed you
with ephemera before you can object.

# Ordinary Grace

thunder & rain last night
this morning growth comes as a shock
the heightened green of the grass

a new generation of insects
even the trees appear loftier
overhead the deep flapping of galahs

the amorous prattle—there is no language

of the holy I tell the birds
as they dip & wheel the sun hitting
the soft gray of their wings

& flashing their pink undersides as I sink
into the green & watery
vernacular of the natural world

# The Nightgown

Reason is dream turned inside out
so we see daylight's other side

or is it the other way round—
dream is reason turned inside out

as the Japanese woman in her desire
turns her nightgown inside out

to dream of her absent lover—
constructs of seams and loose threads

facing the world, the seeming seamless
elision of silks against her flesh

in daylight she watches her body age
(the long rains are falling)

commits to a life of dreaming—
whether the lover appears or he doesn't

whether their meeting is fruitful or isn't—
the black shell of night is a nut or is not.

# The Poet's Bed

The sheets have been changed
since she lay here, maybe even the mattress,
but the frame remains the same:
the head and foot composed of white
metal bars topped with brass bulbs
and a penchant for creaking
each time I shift my body's sleepless weight

kept awake by the stroke of her fist
dragging in fits across the page as she writes in bed,
her ribcage rattling as her inner weather
turns wintry: evidence
that objects do absorb the sounds
of their history: as with the floors of Dachau

where a sensitive must press the heels
of her palms against her ears: not to drown
the agony of screams—there weren't any—
but to drown the world silence
that accompanied the barefoot shuffle.

Mother of my art, it is time
I made amends: too long I have blamed you for
not needing to live, as desperately as I do.
It is arrogant of the living to command the dead:
to be different than you were in life,
to bless me and yourself,
but if you were here with me, awake
and chilled by the sudden voice of the wind,
maybe you could walk with me
or come after to see what I had seen, which was
nothing: only shadows
long and blue on the silvered night floor.

## Seferis

Every day carried away more & more
by this drunkenness. The sea. The mountains
dance without moving—I'm crazy
about the trees in this light. The sea
is breathless—without a ripple—pine
needles motionless as sea-urchins
in clear depths. Writing this I'm drunk
on it all. A black ship trawls
the horizon. There is a sense that if
the slightest crack opened up in this faultless
scene, all things would spill out beyond
the four points of the horizon & leave me
naked, alone & begging for alms. I hate knowing
my life will not be long enough.

## The Angel and the Hermit

It is the fashion of the age
to believe that behind nature's cruelest acts
lie the secret springs of divine tenderness and love.
As when the angel rose in the night
to strangle his host's infant son asleep in the cradle,
we are to see (as the hermit did)
that the birth of the son had made the father covetous,
breaking commandments in order
to heap up treasures, which the boy-had-he-lived
would have wasted in idle debauchery.
By this act that seemed so cruel
the angel saved both parent and child.
Likewise the woman buying oranges this morning
told the fruiterer the blessing
in her daughter's death was that the children
became close to their father and more independent.
How the angel's hand must have gleamed
with holy purpose as he stroked their mother's breast,
the cells in her glands drawn to his touch
like metal filings to a magnet.
Perhaps she thought it was her husband's touch
that made her rise, chilled, and catch the dark body
of swallows departing the lawn.
What if the angel had lingered and seen
not the first grail of light on her hair,
but the way her husband remembered the scene
months later and alone
with a grief more ancient than flowers and graves?
What if the man, looking up
from his pain, saw tears in the eyes of an angel
and, unflinching, reached out,
as nightly he reached out to his children,

filled not with forgetting but deep remembering,
his body alive with tenderness not to be found
in books or false sermons but the fierce
tenderness of one who will try anything to survive.

# Love Begins with a Vision

think of a swallow's wheeling
        flight flaring out
like a flamenco dancer's skirt

        or think of an aircraft flaring
nose tipped up
        to slow before landing

but before this
        think of the birds themselves
swallows swimming fast

        a few inches above
fresh-turned soil
        fanning their wing and tail feathers

flaring upward for
        a long still moment to pluck
an insect from the air

# The Photograph

I did not stay on that mountain,
in the shabby A-frame
with its dusty porch and torn screen door,
the pine needles and snow
I'd track in on my boots,
the leaky, potbelly stove that smoked,
more than it heated, everything
I owned—my hair, my skin—
smelling of charred orange wood;

and the dark attic bedroom
with its single window that, while making
love, I could look through: cedar tips
and copper catkins that, Octobers, billowed—
clouds of pollen refracting further
the already bowed alpine light,
coating my window sill, the world below, yellow
like a plague from a Marquez novel
making me forget my name, my history,
my boundaries—

                I can no longer
look at us sitting in that photograph
on a dusty porch in California—
you reading *Love in the Time of Cholera*
for your second time; and me, *One Hundred Years
of Solitude*. Above us blue acres
of mountain sky. Daffodils bloom in the snow.
The shadow of your dog curls at my feet.
Reaching for our beers, our fingers touch
and entwine. In the photograph
we don't ever let go.

# Christmas Day

*Cuzco, Peru*

Even the bells of San Blas cannot wake
him. Nor the smell of gunpowder that lifts
from the streets with the rain. Nor Camilla's crying
at dawn, *Feliz Navidad!* Nor my breasts
as they press into his back. He is fast asleep and I
am practicing detachment. His neck is scarlet,
sunburnt from yesterday's *siesta* in the Plaza
de Armas and already his skin is starting to shed,
to roll at the edges like the pages of an old
book. Underneath he is brand new. I take a piece
of skin and carefully peel it down his neck. It
detaches in the shape of a parabola—billows
like a little sail—and tears abruptly at the tip. I
hold up my relic to the light: it is clear
like cellophane and dries to a cloudy white. I
am wanting my *caballista*, but he is not in his skin:
it is only his wrapping! He must be underneath. I
peel faster. I want to uncover him. He
is my Christmas present. I want to open
him. I shake him. I want to hear what's inside. I
roll him over and peel back his eyes.

# Routine Love Poem

### 1

they make & remake coffee
they make & remake the bed

he brushes her hair from her eyes
he says: my love

she was afraid to want more

they make & remake coffee
they make & remake the bed

what can she do, he has touched her
here & here & here

what can she do, he touched her
she was afraid to want more


### 2

they make & remake coffee
they make & remake the bed

he inhales & settles
his cigarette on the edge of the sink

brushes her hair from her eyes
he says: my love

what can she do, she has opened
her eyes as he balanced above her

bent down to kiss her mouth
what can she do, she has opened

she has opened


3
they make & remake coffee
they make & remake the bed

the sun hits the kitchen
she sits on his lap & he touches her

here & here & here

what can she do, she can hear herself
in the scream of the kettle

he says: isn't this your life

what can she do, she can hear
herself in the scream

demanding more air, more light


4
they are in the dark
in the beginning of a movie

the camera frames a long shot

a man & woman perform
the routine gestures of breakfast

toast, coffee, newspaper

the camera goes in on the woman
she crosses her legs

& fingers her wedding ring

things do not turn out in the end
they turn & turn


5

what can she do, now that she is lost
in the bed

what can she do, now that the sheets
have fallen

now the blanket is on the floor
the mattress exposed

now her hair is not in her eyes
now that there aren't any words

her hair is his

she is lost, he has touched her
here & here & here


6

they are in the dark again
he strikes a match & inhales

his cigarette shapes
& reshapes his body

liberates his wrist
& inflames the narrative

she says: the truth
is I will not follow you

he says: of course
& smokes his cigarette

down to the end


    7
they make & remake coffee
they make & remake the bed

he exhales & extinguishes
his cigarette

turns the television off

she inhales & closes her eyes
she says: what can I do

they are in the dark

he balances above her
bends down to kiss her mouth

he says: isn't this your life

# California Morning

We're restless again, you and I, up
at six stacking split pine out of the rain.

Your man's left again leaving fresh-cut
dreadlocks, no note, in a shoebox

beside your bed. Another morning-
mourning pile, I call it, because he arranges them

at dawn to hurt you. You're thinking you'll go
to Bordeaux again or maybe Senegal

and I'm thinking Havana or anywhere. Our dreams
are distant and rife with living as the waters

of a tropical sea. Earlier I think I heard you
cry but then the sounds from things

that won't be pinned are quickly gone.

## Festival of the Sun

Last night
the way he held me
seemed especially sweet
my body wracked
with influenza
my skin wet
as if doused with alcohol
& lit. I shivered
as he held my wrists
above my head & told me
*you are not cut off*
*from the sun*
turning my world
upside down
I was a condor
the sky's heaviest bird.

## Woman Holding a Vase

It is terrifying to think
how long I must be Léger's *Woman
Holding a Vase*—bright enamel
on stretched canvas—all my longing locked
into a brushstroke. It's terrifying to think
how long I must stand here—
my back against the wall—arranging
flowers, as I arrange my lovers,
in a pattern of forgetfulness:
I who does not forget easily.
There must be an art—a correct procedure
at least—to letting memory devolve
into indifference. But what do I know?
I am Léger's *Woman*. My breast
is a blue circle—a simple shape
asserting itself—my limbs and joints
are cardboard cutouts outlined in black
like Medieval stained glass.
I have no gift for this forgetting.
I could have been a type or symbol,
a road or astrological sign,
a happy robot or cheerful paper doll
inflating into a pneumatic toy
naively posed like 1950s soft-core porn.
I could have been a caryatid
from the Erechtheion, a female column
upholding the entablature,
or a Cycladic fertility doll exciting
heathen loins to lust. But no.
I am Léger's *Woman* learning to forget—
the better to be a futurist—learning to love
the machine for its motion and speed,
its compliance and fidelity.
Hanging here, I can look forward

to the future—the geometries
of things to come—carrying lightly
the weight of my nostalgia,
rejoicing in my catalepsy, celebrating
only myself—my chic design, my sheen,
my sheet metal surface, my fact of being,
my heroic act of forgetting—arranging flowers
with timeless jazzy optimism.

# Where is the Love?

Under the solemn mantle of darkness

In the belly of a bloated toad

In the green stuff that fills the tissues that conjure light into air

Gone with the dragons who so long lorded it over the hemispheres

Lounging with cloud shadows on a jade lake

Trapped in an embryonic history where it darts to and fro, through the waves, with the prophecy of a vertebrate skeleton inside it

Off to witness the lemmings suicide

Out the gate and onwards to fathom the infinite

In the notes of a sympathetic critic who has filed it for reference under a glass of water

In Paris, where its long life is worthily ended amid words and deeds of affectionate homage

Sitting at a table where was written the most perfect prose that ever flowed from a pen and looking about the little room with its evidences of plain living and high thinking

Rising in pitch until it is too acute for the human ear to cognize and thus vanishing from consciousness

In the void created when the thumb and forefinger touch in a token of contemplative ecstasy

In the battle cry *may you live ten thousand years*

## Tomorrow I Will Plant Flowers,
## Find a New Place to Hang My Keys

I have no body only belongings.
The women, midwives at my disappearance,

remove old tapestries from the walls
and clean some old yellow teacups

with broken edges. I stop to contemplate
the cups. They remind me of bodies

that, after making love, shine
with lost desire. They smell of travel

and refuge. The women wrap the cups
in the tapestries and put them in my suitcase.

I have loved these cups and cared for them
because, in them, I have steeped the tea

for so many exiles. Bright bodies full
of fragrance and bits of orange.

# Palinode

I have written before how I loved him
but I have never written how I disliked him too.
A Romani psychic said shallow and stingy
and I blinked and recognized his sign.
He'd flirt with waitresses then turn to me bored.
After a fight I flew across an ocean and a continent
to see him and he saw me once. I listened
to his endless fears of my supposedly impending
infidelity and in thirteen months he'd done it first.
He was allergic to everything—my cat, my dust,
my cooking left him red-eyed and apologetic
as he drove home sneezing. I didn't mind
the drink and smoke but his weakness when he
pledged to quit and couldn't made me turn away
embarrassed. He was more knowledgeable
than intelligent. He read the same books over
and over and raged when I skipped the dull bits.
He corrected my grammar during long distance
phone calls. He scarcely mentioned my poems.
One night in Bucharest he denied I beat him
at backgammon so I hit him with a pillow. He fell
to the mattress laughing, his body convulsing
around the pillow, and I asked what is so funny.
He said, you. I am just so happy with you.

## Insufficient Knowledge

You have to start with insufficient knowledge,
yes, this, and yes, praise be, then this,
you have to have that kind of courage.

A breath, a step, a word: it's to your advantage
to begin. There isn't time to wait for grace—
you have to start with insufficient knowledge.

Think of the first human to sail over the edge
of the world, or a base jumper departing an edifice:
you have to have that kind of courage.

Break your fists, your back, your brain, punch
yourself an opening. This is all there is:
you have to start with insufficient knowledge

of the heart, that higher organ, which
from time to time catches us by surprise
and we startle with the kind of courage

that will spend it all, not hold back, wage
everything, all, right away, every time, yes.
You have to love with insufficient knowledge,
you have to have that kind of courage.

# The Cairn

*Mount Warning, New South Wales*

You look to me for answers

but I know nothing: I am simple stone
conscripted with a leaf into a human

sign. I promise you I solve nothing.
I am mere punctuation to alert you
to juncture and entrance. Check yourself:

are you where you should be by now?
where did you mean to be and how far
have you strayed? I concede to follow me
might bring disaster but can you afford

to ignore my improbable height?
Had a strong wind toppled me or
an animal bungled too close you might
have been saved this interminable doubt

you might have walked blithely to your end
never suspecting the error in your path.
Now here you are, mid-point in your journey,
questioning a stone of your origins and destination.
Bronwyn, it is not in my make up to pity you.
Make a decision and be on your way.

# Homecomings

Pretend there still are homecomings.
That we still have homes and can find them.
Pretend home is more than the meridian
encircling heart and soil at birth,

more than a history of receding horizon,
more than the illusion left behind.
Pretend it is more. There is a woman,
she could be anyone, sitting at her desk

or in a library, lying in somebody's bed
or her own. She is studying maps—the clock-
wise swirl of oceans, migration of sands,
the continents' roam—but she cannot find

a map to suit her: one unpinned by stasis,
by longitude's tall bar or latitude's cross-
hatching. Her hand is following the curve
of equator trying to get back to a beginning,

but her fingers are falling off the page,
learning the measurement of loss,
of never the absolute, of nowhere a finality.
Her mind swerves on its axis and her face

is pressed into the page—she is pretending
it is a lover's neck, and the scent of paper
and ink is walking her back to the mulga,
back to spinifex plains and uncontoured sky.

Here, there is nowhere to go. Except to the bush
pomegranate and the gnarled track of its branch.
Her hand is open but reaching for the flower—
burnt orange petal—as if it were fruit.

# My Nepenthe

By some act of choice,
the mid-vein extends
beyond its leaf into vine;
green umbilicus
undulating through sun-
light then u-turning
to uphold an urn,
an organ of predation,
usurping the roots
in its greed to survive.
Sweet nectar on the lip—
an insect in love with
the pink of the mouth,
sips a while then slips,
step by long step
down the slick passage
of the waxed and dew-
dappled throat, retreat
barred by delicate hairs
that pitfall the prey
into a pool of acid rain,
to drown and steep
amid the dissolving
carcasses of flies
and the white skeleton
of a frog. If ever again
I am asked to explain
myself, I will point to
the moment this mid-
vein rejects the confines
of its leaf and say: *this.*
*I am this.*

# Original Sin

Right before she died Rita said, *if
I could live my life over again, I would
have more sex and fewer children,*
and I believed her in Laguna Niguel,
sitting cross-legged at that French bistro,
ordering chocolate cake called *Original
Sin*, the pink rising in her English
cheeks like rice paper taking up the ink
as she stared down the seven layers
of bitter-sweet wafer melded together
with cream and strawberries and floating
in a pool of hot maple-syrup.
*Fuck my diabetes,* she whispered
as the handsome waiter left, *I'm eating.*
I can see her, a teenage girl again,
lying among the backyard strawberries,
this time to take her childhood sweetheart
now that she knows how: her heels
and shoulders, his elbows and knees pressing
into the loam, her back arched and falling
like a bridge. I can see her a young wife
standing in her kitchen, sipping scotch
and lifting her skirt for her husband
after work, her small hands gripping
the porcelain taps while he takes her
from behind. And the next morning,
arranging silk chrysanthemums in a vase,
then pushing aside the coffee table
with her foot to straddle her husband's best
friend on the floor while her only child
studies at school. And years later,
after all the suffering, after all his cheating
and her own, I am not surprised
to see Rita returning to her marriage bed,

her hands brushing the dry length
of her husband's limbs as if with flour,
kneading his soft muscle, their tongues
mingling with embarrassment, the shy
awkwardness of a man and woman
who have slept beside each other for forty-
five years making their hate
known and not remembering why.

## Miserability

Grey skies over Brisbane today—
maybe like the skies over St Petersburg,
I think, but she says *no*.
*The clouds in St Petersburg are heavy like bells.*
And so it is with her eyes.
*Your people are kind*, she says, *this is true*
*but because I know how it is*
*to be whittled down to a twig & grow again into a tree—*
*because I know it & speak it,*
*they think me clown.*
Yes, I say, my people are kind
but we do not like to talk about sad things.
It's always been this way.
She looks at me through wet lashes
in that wounding way of children,
her black eyes bright with *miserability*—
*Then tell me*, she says, as if I were her
messenger & not her witness, *where are your poets?*

# Monologue on Bob Hope Blvd

Firm hand, he says, holding mine.
His name is Arthur Kippling,
and he must be strong to have survived

his wife's nursing home. He couldn't
shut her up, and the nurses would call him
at all hours when he was at home

feeling lonesome. *She just keeps*
*screaming*, they said over and over.
He was a schoolteacher, retired in '74,

moved to Desert Hotsprings in '75.
He's traveled a lot, seen every continent,
every state capital in Australia

except Darwin. He even went
to Alice Springs and saw an Aborigine
with a captivating face, and he thought

to ask first if he could take
the man's picture, and the man said *yes,*
*but for a dollar*. His wife just died

less than a month ago.
She'd had a stroke seven months before.
Lucky are the ones who go quickly.

She deteriorated every day,
and every time he left the nursing home
he thought it would be his last time

to see her. His doctor put him on
antidepressants, but he doesn't know
if they're working, and referred him

to a psychotherapist just to talk,
because he was married forty-five years,
and it wasn't a happy marriage

but it was a long time. What he needs
is a *Born Again Pagan* sticker
for his daughter. She won't put it on

her bumper, but she'll keep it
in the house. He should have bought it
when first he saw it at a little shop

called *Avalon*, but he didn't.
I wonder if you can help me, he says,
this is what I'm looking for.

# The Flood

What do they know of war
it's the summer of 1938
and they're smiling on a beach
in Tenby, Wales. History
hasn't happened yet, though Freud's
rocked up in London, Superman debuted
in Action Comics #1, and Roosevelt
has commenced his fireside chats.
But it's a dazzling black and white
chromogenic day in Tenby, and Frank
is solid in white linens,
sleeves rolled up, Havana at hand,
sand scalloping his white patent shoes.
Elsie leans in for a kiss,
tanned in a halter top and shorts,
she touches his forearm
with an intimate lightness that reveals
no knowledge of the future—at least
that's how I remember

the photograph
as it sat near a century away
on my window sill in Brisbane,
Australia. Now I kneel
at a bathtub and everywhere
around me faces stare up
from the mud. Frank and Elsie
float into the present. I wash them
with my thumbs as tenderly
I washed sleep from the eyes
of their granddaughter and a huge red
beam, curtain of fire, Aurora
Australis, blooms across Wales,
lighting up their lives from the other side

of death. And the brain can discern
the different scales of loss—
it's paper in my hands not flesh—
but the heart, the biological
heart—how the heart pounds
at what it takes, and almost hopes,
is history's end.

# One of the Horses of Marly

*Guillaume Coustou, 1745*

Human, stop this circling round
& around the same mistakes,
urging my heart forward with your heels
& your big want. Surely you must

get tired of racetracks & carousels,
careering for salvation while your ghost
gnaws on a rock. Look at you,
sowing and reaping your hatred,

the same barren crop your father milled
with your mother's bones & son's heart
to make sop for his sins. Face it,
whatever you mean to love you destroy:

nothing gets by your spinning net,
your lust for revolution, in your craving
even the thrashing cycle of your self
becomes your quarry. If you would

just give me my head I could take you
home to bloodless plains, I could
transform your warring with a straight
line into miraculous fraternity. O

human too dizzy to see, you shoot
an arrow & it stabs you in the back.

# Contemplating Chaos at Burleigh Heads

My daughter skips
a jellyfish across the flats. She is collecting
pippies in a bucket and wears wet flowers
in her hair. It occurs to me
that my entire reality is reduced to ideas
of trees, stones and animals. That
the daughter I see ordinarily
is only the representation of an abstraction: a category
of sex, a name, a description, a series
of events—

       the flowers in her hair
are not flowers. They are drowned butterflies
that have washed up with the jellyfish
along the shore—

       and for that matter,
am I not an abstraction to myself? Gesturing
at the funnels and rolls of my emotions
with words like *fear, joy*, or *grief*. The grief
that comes when I confront my enormous uncertainty
about who this child is.

She crouches
at the water's edge watching the waves
wash over her feet. If I could bend
a thread around the craggy line
of her body, trace her bays
and indentations, the slender peninsulas
of her fingers and toes, trace every drift
and ripple down to the twists and turns
of her molecules, the coastline
of her body would be infinite. And
because her body constantly erodes and renews

it would be an infinity that constantly
changes.
          Soft snores float
from her bedroom. I stop writing
and walk outside. A smell of humus,
flash of silky oaks, the shadow of a possum crashes
along the gutter. Soon it will rain.


Yesterday,
driving home from the beach,
I studied her in glances as she slept.
Each view varied so that—how do I say this?—
I saw first one child,
then another and another like a shuffling
of snapshots. But after some time,
I discovered a child that exists
between a possibility of several children.

I reached over
and touched that child's cheek: it was hot and red
and dented beneath my fingers.


          It begins to rain.


When I return to my desk,
she will bring me the pippies in her bucket. A spray
of sand will cling to her feet and ankles,
her every step towards me eroding the surface
of her skin, leaving remnants of her
cells among the sand's fragments of shells
and corals.

# Girls' Night of Long Island

We drink vodka martinis
with tiny onions and green olives,
eat popcorn and salty pork and talk
about circumcision. That's their problem,
we decide, their insecurity, the root
of their castration anxiety. Teresa laughs,
she's not complaining,
she thinks it's worth the sacrifice.
I shrug, fixing another drink, either way.
'What does she care?' Ruth asks,
'She's Australian!' and everybody laughs.
But Meg is happy at least one
woman's not fussy
because when her premature son
was born they stuck dozens of tubes
into his little red body,
and when he came out of ICU,
she just decided, forget it. Ruth says
it was the same with her son,
though longer ago,
his lung burst in the delivery room—
from a resuscitator set at adult pressure—
and they took him to another hospital
to have the lung re-inflated.
For a week she cried,
without her child or any visitors,
and when she finally got him back,
she wouldn't let another doctor
touch him. And besides,
she laughs chewing on an olive,
all of her grandparents
and all of her uncles and all of her aunts
died at Auschwitz,
and she thought about this,

as she suckled her newborn son,
that if another Hitler came to power
at least he wouldn't get
this little Jew. And her words fall heavy
on the living room, just like the rain
falling outside. Meg is asleep.
Her second martini too much
after half a Xanax. Some of us turn
to the fire. Some of us turn
to the rain.

## Lord Duke

So there you are in New Orleans
three weeks before Mardi Gras
sitting naked in 80 degree Fahrenheit heat
listening to public radio jazz 24/7
in a shotgun shack in an all black neighborhood
front & back doors open
let the breeze come cool you down
"It's January somewhere."
And your rent just $250/m for a house
all to yourself: granted
your closet is something akin to a bank safe
& you sleep with a loaded 9mm
tucked beneath your pillow. But it's quiet,
at least, your house stuck between
two sides of the same graveyard
& next door five refrigerator-sized black
brothers to look over you. Five blocks
away the streetcar that rides right down the middle
of NOLA's richest greenbelt—St. Charles Ave—
carries you to the French Quarter
where nights you sit in Internet cafés
crying truckloads over the pretty entomologist
you left behind in Albuquerque. Again.
She wanted a marrying man & you
decided for the third time it weren't gonna
be you. Duke, last night I dreamed
the mighty Mississippi wrapped its long arm
around you in a drunken embrace & trashed your heart
like a junkyard aquarium.

# Leaving West End

At the bus stop,
the woman in the Laura Ashley dress
and combat boots
leans the blunt line of her fringe
against her boyfriend's chin.
He bites his lower lip—thrusting
the silver stud that punctures his chin—
and looks down the white line
of her center part to his future
ten minutes from now or before.
His arms wrap around her waist,
crossing at the wrists,
and his palms rest on the high haunches
of her buttocks.
I don't think I have ever been held
quite like that.
They are too young, I think,
to have questioned love,
if it is all that it is cracked up to be,
but by the raven color
of the woman's dyed hair, I imagine
she might have read Baudelaire,
her favorite book,
*Confessions of An Opium Addict.*
Last night, on the phone,
my friend told me she smoked heroin
with her girlfriend—it was like
turning her veins inside out, she said,
so the velvet was on the outside.
All night, she said,
their bodies coiling each other
like smoke at its sexiest
and, making love, she can't remember
if she came, but she remembers

wondering if she might.
And what's the matter with that,
she said, she has a good job
and makes a lot of money.
My bus pulls up and I climb on
leaving the man and woman
locked together on the footpath.
Through the window, I watch
the woman look up
to kiss her boyfriend, slipping
the pink of her tongue
into his mouth, her kohl-rimmed eyes
open and staring,
searing black holes onto my retinas
like a shadowgraph of lovers
burnt onto a city wall.

# Deep Creek Hot Springs

This sanctuary has shriveled
from what it was—its Indians have fled,
and its healing lies limp and unused.
Still we say, *this is a power place,*
as we wade through the shallows
with the little fish nibbling at our ankles,
past the German beauty sitting naked
on a boulder and speaking of *abundance*
while her American admirer captures
her unclothed sermon on video.
And after we make love beneath a dying oak,
we sit in the hotspring where the German beauty sat,
and you tell me of the Mexican busboy
who said his twenty-year marriage passed
like ten minutes—adding after a calculated
pause—*underwater*. And I smile,
feeling the spring's heat rip through me
like a buzz saw, smiling as the clear green water
slices your white legs in two.

# Crows

Let me be part of the outrageous chaos,
dawn brawl breaking light. Shakescene. Upstart.
Cashing in on air. Here

above crazed concrete, tap roots and leaf-rot
I hear crows croak and fly back
and forth, clear of roofs and back-lit pines,

clear of vision. I don't know
what *soul* is exactly, but I think
crows might have it: hip hop rap and black
music, throat feathers puffed in dark song—

now I am afraid
my hearing untranslates the morning. Ear-phlegm.

Mind-gap. How to be
faithful to the crow-stepped branch, how to write
crow-scent in a human score?

Now one crow catches my ear.
I love how he appears to have no love
of melody, not a bar of music scratched into his brain.

I want to know
what can be made of this racket,
my ear scanning each syllable of the sky until dawn

becomes dimensional
and the crow becomes itself,
perched on a high branch of a hind tree

I see only with my ear—the aural world giving
him feedback, shrieking like a microphone
too close to a speaker
and exploding into applause.

# Driving Into Distance

### 1

The poet says that the psychologist says, that
the anthropologist says, that when one person
envisions another, the image takes form in the
mind at a distance of about 10 feet. It is as if
even the *idea* of *thou* is a threat. And somehow
this seems important.

### 2

Today, leaving Tahoe, it seemed all of life
was headlonging me: cars, cyclists, joggers,
horses, rivers, mountains all pushing their way
into me and I—for all my layers—was
defenseless as a diary confession. I said *I love
you* thinking I was creating enormous intimacy
using an *I*, but instead, his *thou* backed off
as my *I* moved in to inhabit. Language,
it seems, misrepresents me: the *I* bending
its tyranny into an argillaceous loop, running
circles around desire, until the self is a Mobius
strip and *I love you* a cruel equation equaling
a snowdrift between us.

### 3

Somewhere south of Bakersfield, a swarm
of butterflies colored the air above the road-
side cabbages a fragile yellow: ten thousand
wings over I-5, tacking against the wind,
striking my windshield in silent syncopation.
It was oddly beautiful, these little losses.
And it makes sense that we use our subjectivity
to distend our inward space, our solipsism

reconfiguring the body, extenuating time,
as if to inhale the synthetic rose saying *this way,
it will last forever.*


4

At home I found a yellow butterfly stuck
in the fender, its life inaudible except
for the slow fanning of wings. I stared into
the frailty of its body against the hard
metal fender to which it clung, mapping
myself onto its labyrinth of yellow, laboring
like the insect to survive, to let go. I wanted
to cup its life like my palm around a match.
And as I stroked the narrow isthmus
between east and west wing, a silence fell
from its body not unlike the silence
that descends from arching grasses or clings
to mountain snow.


5

I remembered the story he told me
of the runner from Montana and the gunman
who ran behind her to protect her from
*what?* The body breaking up? It was oddly
beautiful, he said. And as my mind traversed
the frightened space between runner
and gunman, I was thinking of those ten
foot distances between desire, longing for
that unsounded moment when language will
stop, concentric rings of thought collapsing
like a medicine cup, and I can settle
into the soundness of him: my *I* in *thou.*

6

I guess at some point I want to live
contently in the body of another. *There, it is
said.* But what can be said to the
anthropologist? Or the psychologist? Except
to say—sometimes there is solace
in a vantage point and comfort in a vista;
an odd beauty in a lover's hand as it waves
*good-bye* across the sky and relinquishes.
In his hand now—somewhere
in the distance—open and soft
as he sleeps.

## Grandiflora

It was a rose with a grandiose name
—a *grandiflora*—a thoroughly modern rose
in a black plastic bucket,
US patent #6725 strapped to its ankle
and a note from my lover
pressed to a thorn: *I know you'll let it die.*
*Please don't let it die.* All summer long
my rose bush trembled with living,
pale pink buds tighter than infant fists
unfurling into fragrant ruffles,
fold on fold of petal aching into bloom,
a scent of fresh tea and honey rising
and curving like a hawk
leaning into nothingness only to fade
and fall in a soft detonation
of memory. I should have watered it more
or cut it back before winter,
but I left it to stomach the cold,
its leaves curling like arthritic fingers,
its flowers crunching underfoot.
And when spring arrived and no leaf buds
appeared on its brittle spine,
I took my shears and cut and cut and cut.
I was searching for some meaning,
for some hidden living,
or even a moment or two of green,
but my *grandiflora* was just a dead inch
in a black plastic bucket,
its license around its toe like a dog tag.
And it doesn't matter that it was from him,
the last gift he gave me.
This time, it's not about him.

# Ars Poetica

I used to want
to say one thing

& have it turn

out to be another.
Now I only want

to say one thing.
As if the pleasure

now is in the voicing
not the trickery

but the soul making
itself heard

above the traffic.

# Found Wanting at
# Zen Mountain Monastery

*ichi*

He is sitting by a wall.
He cannot see the cherry trees
or my skirt as it billows
in the wind. His molecules
are senseless and lacking
in compulsion as clouds that
have spilled their rain.


*ni*

At lunch a Japanese woman tells me
she has just buried her drowned son.
After the funeral, her husband left
with their dead son's relief teacher.
He had never known love like this.
He has only one life to live, he said.
He was asking for her blessing.
The first night in her empty house,
she dreamt her mind was muddled,
that she had buried her husband
and blessed her son.


*san*

Desire or craving, he says
(he means to say thirst),
is the cause of all suffering.
(He is the one who will
not remember me more,
the one who lets my face fall
without shock like vapor
from his mind.)

*shi*
So the woman fired up her motorbike,
rode through the hills to the monastery,
left her credit card with the office monk
and walked into the *zendo*. Her mind
was empty. Her body composed as
the ashed mantle of a kerosene lantern.


*go*
Some of us have bodies
so spongious thin and
delicate that we are fed
only by sucking
in some fine spirit
liqueur that pierces like
pure air and pine oil.


*roku*
"You have a question?" the Roshi asks
the woman a week later.
"It is difficult living two lives," she says.
"Two lives?"
"Yes. One life as it should be,
the other as it is."
"You would like only one life?" Roshi asks.
"Yes."
"So you feel you must pick one?"
"Yes."
"Pick the life in which flowers grow in dirt."

*nana*
The one I love
is sitting by a wall.
The wall is white.

# Memory

Will it ever end?
Only from underneath,
my hand reaching
through the backyard cedar,
scooping up koi,
orange in the blackened pond,
the wind in my hair,
I could live as the *tillandsia*—
on air, I think,
on the breath of a word.
No it will never,
not even underneath.

# Port Moresby

I am squatting on the steps
a red hibiscus in my hair

my skin at ten is not yet ravaged
by years of light

I turn away as the camera clicks
on the steps leading

to the glass door with a row of blue
swallowtail decals

to stop us smashing through

soon things will happen
I will survive but not fully

recover from the break ins
breakups the break

downs and it will all happen
here in this teeming

white light that washes
the features from my face and glints

off my kneecap like a bullet

# A Rush of Butterflies

Jacaranda—still
purple after all these years—
higher in the sky.

        Leaves of two trees almost touch—
        far below their roots embrace.

Losing you I prune
the bright red leaf tips—my breast
aching from hedging.

        Still no word from you—I write
        eighteen haiku about loss.

By my foot, a skink
fixes an eye on me—more
devoted than you.

        My shovel splits an earthworm—
        I watch the two ends wriggle.

Recalling the blue
of your unwashed comforter—
white with wet semen.

        A dewdrop falls from its leaf—
        today I drop the fight.

Moon or not, moss hugs
a rock. See how I loved you?
See how I loved you?


Behind a hill, the sun falls—
a sky bled and left to die.


On my knees—dead flies
along the skirting—the hard
wood floor reflects me.


Towels bone dry on a clothesline—
going on seven days now.


A fig leaf trembles
on its back, its skin like lace
slipping into dust.


A rush of spring butterflies—
all of life passes me by.


Quick! Think something else:
pollen in leather sandals
by the open door.


Even as it rains,
the spider respins its web.

# The Isurumuniya Lovers
*Anuradhapura, 5th Century AD*

Each minute of the season we polished
like a silver coin, the two of us together

in our wantonness. You were sheer
& undeniable as hunger, down a thermal

like a hawk, you descended in a gust
to bring me gifts from deep inside

the past. Each night I found the present
tense of you. Your body on the bed

conducting light, the little room lit up,
my sex ransacked by a branch

of burning sky. Something akin to a bird
broke a hole in the heart of my body

& the earth gave out its full muffle
of mind in which no thought ran clear,

nothing was clear, except the sweet flood
between us. Something awakened

& something breathed more deeply.
I dreamed that underneath the lake

there was another lake & when I woke
everything that had been hidden

was unhidden. Each stone in the gravel
path made known its name, lichen flared

on the temple tree by the terrace
& carp wrapped in shadow followed us

through sunlit depths. Each morning
we walked in staggered silence

until the future came
to blind us with its mirror.

# Graffiti on the Mirror Wall

*Sigiriya, 7–11th Centuries AD*

I came and saw the girls with gold chains
between their breasts—now heaven is no good

o

Ladies like you make the hairs
of men like me stand up and beg

o

That doe-eyed mountain woman pisses me off—
string of pearls in her hand, air of rivalry in her body

o

Light from their bodies
like the moon wanders in the cool wind

o

I am Lord Sangapale and I wrote this song:

We spoke but they wouldn't listen, those mountain ladies
gave us not even a twitch of an eyelash

o

This lady, a tender bud, spoke to me with the flower in her hand.
It is therefore a lie that the ladies do not speak

o

Even here the stanzas won't come: I am heartsick
in the mist of the golden ones

o

Lady, give up your sorrow—
what else can be said beyond the poem?

o

Song of Poyalmi, Balath Palace Guard:

Forgive me. Long Eyed One of the Mountain—
having come here, having seen, death no longer troubles me

o

Look at the long-eyed one, but do not sing to her
or she will haunt your heart forever

o

I saw the nymphs standing in heaven
and my hand jumped up to grasp their gauze

o

Song of Kithalu of Ruhunu:

When he thought the ladies without their men could be his,
his happiness doubled to see the golden ones on the mountainside

o

The girl with golden skin pleases the mind—
as for her breasts I see swans drunk on nectar

o

Youth is crushed by age, the body sickens, life departs—
but here stands, as it were, the unafflicted

o

Listen! This is Na Sagasmi,
chief administrator of Budhgamu, writing:

We came to Sihigiri to look at women
and we were not disappointed

# Standing in Bette Davis's Shoes

*Grauman's Chinese Theatre, Hollywood*

You cad!
You dirty swine! No one
has any rights about me except me.
From head to foot, I'm one quivering mass
of loathing. If you could read
my mind you'd shrivel
where you stand. My passions are all
gathered together like fingers that make a fist.
You've the most amazing lack
of humor of anyone I've ever known!
You sound like a book and a very cheap one.
If I wanted to end up in the river
I'd have taken a jump off the Brooklyn Bridge.
If I weren't in such a hurry I'd break right down
and cry. I got things wrong with me
that all the doctors in the world can't fix.
If this is what you call living
I don't want any part of it. I'm humiliated
to the point I must thank you. Some will wind up
in the short end but not me,
baby. If I don't get out of here I hope I die
and burn. There's only one person
in this town that does anybody a real favor.
That's the undertaker—carries them out.
I don't say things nicely. I don't want people
to like me. Nothing pleases me
more than when they don't like me—
means I don't belong. I know all the angles
and I think I'm smart enough to keep one step ahead
of them till I get enough to pack it all in
and live on Easy Street. I don't ask
for things I don't think I can get. I'll get you—
even if I have to crawl back from my grave to do it.

Good! Let's have blood and destruction.
I think I'll have a large order
of prognosis negative. Fasten your seat belts.
It's going to be a bumpy night.

# Feet

When I read of the weeping
feet of Nicholas the Third
I found I already knew

that feet could weep
that there is a weeping
of the whole body

that every pore can bring
forth tears. I'm not sure how
I knew but I knew it early

before things happened—
love, death and other sorrows—
I knew sorrow in the body

before I knew its source.
Outside I expect the cry of doves
but it rains only silence.

# Hand of the Bodhisattva

*India, 1st Century A.D.*

I want to know the ancient palm: how
its lifeline cuts like twine wrapped tightly round
the reel of the hand. I want to know
which hand, dipped in the mind of love, carved

this figure peaceful as a stick of green bamboo:
the lean breast faithful to the heart's simplicity,
diaphragm domed like a woman's long eye,
abdomen stretching below the dhoti's lazy

horizon. The hand calls us into this moment
on which the infinite crosses over into gladness
and we gaze at something singular and joined.
Accept the stone's gift which is not transcendence

but your heart beating at its apprehension.
Here is your life: unlock your fist and begin.

"Seven Feet & Where They're From." This poem began as a response to John Forbes's poem, "Four Heads and How to do Them."

"*Woman Holding a Vase.*" This poem is a dialogue with Cubist painter Ferdinand Léger's 1927 painting of the same name.

"Routine Love Poem." This poem was inspired by a paper presented by Leslie Stern at the University of Queensland, in which she discussed the possibilities in film for creating melodrama through quotidian objects.

"My Nepenthe." Commonly known as "pitcher plant," Nepenthe is a family of carnivorous creepers native to the nutrient-poor peat bogs of Northern Australia and Malaysia. Alternatively, Nepenthe (from the Greek "not" and "grief") is a drug used by the ancients to forget sorrow or turmoil and has come to refer to anything that induces the pleasurable sensation of forgetfulness.

"The Dream." This poem snatches modified phrases from Lance Esplund's review, "Resurrecting Matisse," published in *Harper's Magazine* (December, 2005).

"Memory." *Tillandsia* (commonly known as "air plant") is a family of epiphytes with very small root systems that absorb most of their needed water and nourishment through their leaves. They are sometimes sold glued to pieces of driftwood as curiosities.

"Graffiti on the Mirror Wall." At Sigiriya, Sri Lanka, a highly polished Mirror Wall faces a gallery of frescoes depicting the bare-breasted Sigiriya Maidens. Of an original 500, only 22 have survived. For centuries, kings, noblemen, ladies, monks, guards and laborers wrote graffiti on the Wall in the form of couplets (*muktaka*) addressed to the Maidens. My versions have been constructed using Dr. Senerat Paranavitana's translations in *Sigiri Graffiti* (Oxford UP, 1956).

"Standing in Bette Davis's Shoes." Each sentence is spoken by one of Davis's film characters, variously: Helen Bauer in *Ex-Lady* (1933); Mildred Rogers in *Of Human Bondage* (1934); Joyce Arden in *It's Love I'm After* (1937); Mary Dwight in *Marked Woman* (1937); Judith Traherne in *Dark Victory* (1939); Aunt Charlotte in *The Old Maid* (1939); Regina Giddens in *The Little Foxes* (1941); Maggie in *The Great Lie* (1941); Rosa Moline in *Beyond the Forest* (1949); Margo Channing in *All About Eve* (1950); and Margaret Elliot in *The Star* (1952). On her tombstone is written: "She did it the hard way."

ACKNOWLEDGMENTS

My thanks to the editors of the following publications in which some of these poems previously appeared:

*The Age*, *Antipodes* (US), *The Australian Literary Review*, *Australian Poetry Since 1788* (UNSWP, 2011), *The Best Australian Poems 2007* (Black Inc.), *The Best Australian Poems 2005* (Black Inc.), *The Best Australian Poems 2004* (Black Inc.), *The Best Australian Poems 2005* (Black Inc.), *The Best Australian Poetry 2003* (UQP), *Contemporary Australian Poetry in Chinese Translation* (Shanghai Arts & Literature P, 2007), *Fiddlehead* (Canada), *HEAT*, *Island*, *Journal of Australian Studies*, *Meanjin*, *Motherlode: Australian Women's Poetry 1986—2008* (Puncher and Wattmann, 2009), *The Penguin Anthology of Australian Poetry* (Penguin, 2008), *The Puncher and Wattmann Anthology of Australian Poetry* (2009), *Quadrant*, *Salt: International Journal of Poetry & Poetics*, *The Singapore-Australian Anthology of Poems* (Ethos Books, 2008), *Sixty Classic Australian Poems* (UNSWP, 2009), *Southerly*, *Thirty Australian Poets* (UQP, 2011) and *Windchimes: Asia in Australian Poetry* (Pandanus 2006).

I would like to thank Asialink for a Literature Residency, the Literature Board of the Australia Council for a New Work Grant, and the Eleanor Dark Foundation for a Varuna Writer's Fellowship. My thanks also to Yaddo Artists' Colony, New York, and the Geoffrey Bawa Estate, Sri Lanka, where a number of these poems were written.

Finally I wish to express my gratitude to Paul Kane for his marvelous support during the making of this book: *The Deep North* could not exist without the generosity of his vision.

Bronwyn Lea was born in Tasmania and grew up in Papua New Guinea and the United States. Her books of poetry include *Flight Animals* and *The Other Way Out*, which won the South Australian Premier's Literary Award for Poetry and the Western Australian Premier's Book Award. Her poems have been widely anthologized, most recently in *Australian Poetry Since 1788*; *Thirty Australian Poets*; *Sixty Classic Australian Poems*; and *The Penguin Anthology of Australian Poetry*. In addition, her work has been translated into Chinese, Spanish and Italian. Lea has attended the Squaw Valley Writers workshops in both poetry and fiction, and is the recipient of a Yaddo Fellowship; an Asialink Literature residency at Lunuganga Estate in Sri Lanka; and an Australia Council Literature Residency to work at the B.R. Whiting Studio in Rome. Lea is the founding editor of *The Best Australian Poetry* series and the inaugural editor of *Australian Poetry Journal*. She lives in Brisbane and teaches at the University of Queensland.